Silk Road

Also by Daneen Wardrop

Scholarly Books

Emily Dickinson's Gothic: Goblin with a Gauge
Word, Birth, and Culture in the Poetry of Poe, Whitman, and Dickinson
Emily Dickinson and the Labor of Clothing
Civil War Nurse Narratives, 1863-1870
Crossings in Text and Textile (co-edited with Katherine Joslin)

Books of Poetry

The Odds of Being
Cyclorama
Life as It

Silk Road

Daneen Wardrop

Etruscan Press

Etruscan Press
Wilkes University
84 West South Street
Wilkes-Barre, PA 18766
(570) 408-4546

WILKES UNIVERSITY
www.etruscanpress.org

Published 2018 by Etruscan Press
Printed in the United States of America
Cover image: The Polos Leave Venice from *Li Livres
du Graunt Caam* 1400 © Johannes
Courtesy The Bodleian Library, University of Oxford
Shelfmark: MS. Bodl. 264, fol. 218r
Cover design by Lisa Reynolds
Interior design and typesetting by James Dissette
The text of this book is set in Electra.

First Edition

17 18 19 20 5 4 3 2 1

Library of Congress Cataloging-in-Publication Data

Names: Wardrop, Daneen, 1952- author.
Title: Silk road / by Daneen Wardrop.
Description: First edition. | Wilkes-Barre, PA : Etruscan Press, [2017] |
    Includes bibliographical references.
Identifiers: LCCN 2017045241 | ISBN 9780998750828 (2-8)
Classification: LCC PS3623.A7366 A6 2018 | DDC 811/.6--dc23
LC record available at https://lccn.loc.gov/2017045241

Please turn to the back of this book for a list of the sustaining funders
    of Etruscan Press.

This book is printed on recycled, acid-free paper.

Table of Contents

Acknowledgments

Most of the poems in *Silk Road* have appeared in literary magazines:

Alaska Quarterly Review, Arts and Letters, Barrow Street, Beloit Poetry Journal, Colorado Review, Crazyhorse, Epoch, Green Mountains Review, Gulf Coast: A Journal of Literature and Fine Arts, Madison Review, New York Quarterly

With love and gratitude I thank my family and friends.

I am grateful to Executive Director Philip Brady and everyone at Etruscan Press.

Silk Road

a. A coin-shaped space

When you returned from the far continent

in rags, after twenty years, not recognized,
        jewels sewn in the hems of your Tartar clothes,
                the seams of your clothes highways,

you passed around ginger, ginseng,

                    then jade, lapis—

and I, not then your wife, Marco,
        scorned the jewels reflecting the moon
                but not the moon itself.

The silk road doesn't lead to the moon, you told me.

Every road leads there on some nights,

I said, and then you were following me home—
        brick, tile, marble,

every way leading on till it became vested
        with its own desire for direction—
                walkway, wall, roof.

Did I want *that*, I wonder,
my dress floating to the floor,

        white smoke lifting out the chimney,
                in the distance a shore fluttering like a hem—

You took from your robes

a piece of the Great Kublai Khan's money—
        paper, believe it or not,
                not metal—but big and pannose
            as a veil or handkerchief can hold a face.

Partly to sit here and unfold it, you rode
        through the desert's ear-mirages—
                keening drums and flutes.

You tell me the Great Khan owns *the secret of the alchemists* . . .
      the art of producing . . . paper money—

What your tracks give—the spines of camels, wind-contours in sand—

money gives, unfolds
        need into the world,

a coin-shaped space on your arm where

                in several years, a mole will appear
      that I could never buy but will half believe is half mine.

You tell our daughters about Tartary women

who traded horses, deal in cattle, blankets.

It's good you tell them,
        though they wangle paste beads from their cousins.

On the Great Khan's hunting expeditions, the women
        set up their own tiger-skin tents roped with silk,
                trained their own hawks.

The girls tie scarves on the pavilion and lay down cushions, wheedle
                        into playing hawk
            the cat, who looks, eyes half-hooded, at them.

The women hunted deer with lions and lynxes, sometimes
            eagles, you say, would dive for diamonds.

Our seagulls are edgy above the wharves.
        Now there's one seagull in a whorl of pigeons.

            This is the trick of east : west—

                Some days I am just trying
to prop up morning against evening.

We think we know opulence

by the new ship our city tracks, we toss golden anchors,
                    cut-edged crosses.

When you asked my father for me,

anchors' flukes sharp as salt-blood
clawed the start of the silk road.

As you talked, I sat with mother
                    embroidering an olive tree,

and with permission, you approached
                    as if I were a diadem,

when what I am is a pouring—

How good a business move could it be

to muddy the future? To foretell,
                one should flatter both calendar and customer.

Or, prediction should find a *between*
                        to the parts of time's syntax.

                                  Coiling, the cat,
                sheathed just inside the sill —
at the center of her sleep, untied things

            flap,
                  time is cut —

And the Khan's astrologers wrote predictions —
                    earthquakes, wars, conspiracies —
        on *takuini*, little squares that they would sell
to anyone for small change.

God, *according to his good pleasure, may do more or less*
              than they set down —

      the caveat protecting those who deal in roiling cycles.

The kitty wakes, and with one eye tracks
                a piece of furniture, a spoon, me —

lifts her chin a slice of space off her paws, holds,
        lowers it again.

By such movement do I know we might evade fate

as in tonight, when the couplet of your knees clasps me —

Travelers will come asking for your tales—

        when to discover the world is to digress—
as your *Description* is the book of find and catch,

    instead of cut jewels, the Polo family trade.

You and I know your ghost writer, the romancer, Rustichello,
        peeks out from behind more than just commas—

he's in the giants and chest-headed people—
    more than in between your lashes

when you cut a look at me from across the table
       and shade your eyes,
when you go to view the women behind bright masks
        near the bridge, Ponte de le Tette.

In the cracks between tiles, *spirit voices* keened
      as you rode through night deserts and heard them
         calling you *by name*.

We eat caviar, soups spiced with ginger—
our babies lick Russian honey from their bread.

In the hitch of your eye now I see ease,
      and how can I quarrel with that—

that tale of hunger and ambit—
    and we wipe crumbs from our mouths.

b. Every time I inhale

My youngest wanted to stay in me,

minnows so still
they've turned
water,

she lines me,

wanted to grow
to be woman in me,

eyes, onyx, hair,
princess in part,
in part, fins.

We drink from the canal,

elbows bend forward,
        knees bend back,

neck retracts,

the only way
in,

every time I inhale

I fall into her—

From a balcony I look down to the morning wharf,

where I'm walking through mist dense as bone:
several men hunker there,
faces slack with pipe smoke,
and mine rubbers to the shape—

any shadow—
that it quenches me—
the more razed the more true,

to keep walking, unknowing, passing,

waterfowl tacking—

I want to wrap a wave for a cape
about your shoulders, Marco,
a florid Venetian wave that tides
ermine, pepper, musk, peacock feathers,

though I do not want a wave
that brings African slaves—and your slave, Mongol.

My sight, no bigger than a hand's reach,
I ripple,
and Venice, my face

fractures in the canal:

I pull it out. It comes,
not even dripping—

The child's quick,

a *here,* that drifts—
flash of feather—
not from us,

but from those
who measure measure—
mothers who love their children
for their own bodies.

Dinner meat-smell
catches in loggia arches—

When I take off rings
to dry my hands, they print
on the washstand
water-halos—

I love the crick
in my girl's eyes
as they follow down
my shoulder to arm,

to fingers grown long enough
to hold a city's

flash of columns—

The somewhere, a space,

a gorge
between remorse and promise —
wine and milk —

that I breathe subcutaneously.

Every breath of Mary's

I used to think I could pace

to each of my own.

Why is it given me to walk other's lives before mine?

The ruby made for such fingers? —

The crisp fragrance of apples
made for a breath —

Quest that tempts itself

and petals that tick sky
behind you—

when Rustichello
made you
a knight, you

weren't looking,
he engraved your visor
with sand dunes, camel skulls.

How do you value
kisses next to knights,
next to stories,

next to children,
next to places-in-stories?

Real places.   Cathay.

Story places.   Cathay.

Oh dear, not to be cruel,

but of the worlds,
to give each one
the chance

to whisk-line portraits
of the children, to give

their going-legs the quick
to keep going,

to buy what we tell
with our listening.

I pull my sash tighter,

the neckline pert

but the baby needs me—
and I unlace again—

needs the inside
of inside.

How Rustichello needed Marco
in the keyed room?
Just the two of them,

Marco remembering
the flashing vessels,
the fermented mare's milk
floating over throngs' heads

as the Khan's astrologers
predicted storms by the years—
ox, dragon, dog—

Rustichello wanted the inside
of inside—of that.

I breathe baby,
Rustichello breathed
to make Marco a lord,

make sand a creation,
make an unmade thing a bell?—

stillness existing
only on papyrus—

The canopies of vendors swell to sails

in the Piazza—the bread seller's loaves brown
    and fair as skin, the fruit woman's peaches
        sunsets. Tingly pepper,
the musk of cinnamon a perfectly plucked lute,

        and the note lingers.

I grow more out of breath these days.
The peach vendor bids me rest a minute by her table,
jingles piccolos and ducats, heads and crowns
            in rind-tough hands.

Back at home, travelers come from all maps
        each day to ask Marco for his tellings—
    his stories that keep topping stories.

I can sit next to Marco some days now and no longer miss myself.

Walking past archways,
    strung with a ribboning hand as I pass,
        a child's moue is framed in an arch.

Across from me, the glass blower sits behind his fragile globe.

On a secret island he learned to exhale that orb
        from a blowpipe,
           from ripple to sputter to bubble

to prismed world growing in front of him—

c. Fish-gleams we imagined carats

What some leaders will do for the nonessential,

       to buy spicings, to forget about millet, milk,
so they can worship a god —

          god with a belly full or god with a belly not full —

I straighten the folds of my dress twisted
over the rise again, and also my breasts,
                tightness and rising,
      the mother in me.

Marco was raised.
Kublai Khan too, was raised.

In her sleep my daughter turns sheets of water.

Would that I were Mary, but I'm not, I'm randy, not
                     ready —
     in my bodice lace I tuck a blossom

more blowsy than saviors east or west —

Coins in the fountain shimmer at the bottom,

I look patted in on the water's surface.

The Khan gave rice, millet, and panicum to poor families.
He planted trees by the roadsides because his astrologers wrote,

Those who plant trees are rewarded with long life.

The Khan asked you to send a thousand
        missionaries to China, but the Vatican
                claimed it was consumed with debt,

had no loaves to spread the continent—

        they demurred, missed the chance to convert millions, brinks
                        of millions—
                a road trundling the opposite way
                                        of its feet—

And Buddha, the better bet, stayed—

A little like fresh blood, the smell

of fish rucks up the breeze from the wharf,
      Venice going about its morning,
            thinking about itself going about its morning.

The people of Zardandan wear teeth of gold,
so the city shines gold with every smile
          or wail.

Money: how rich is your trust?

We cast nets to catch fish-gleams we imagined carats,

     and that is Marco's mouth
        when he remembers the twenty years gone,

        for spices first:
            Bengal ginger, cinnamon, spikenard,
            Sichuan salt, galingale,
            Javanese pepper, nutmeg, Zanzibar
            pepper, cloves—

    not for silver or gold, or even silk—

but for the tongue before the fingers,

for the bird stoved in her whistle—

Our daughters' hair, cinnamon scrolls down pillows—

What we know of it at the moment we check before bedtime—

what we know from the cupping, my hand in yours,

                                          sand   salt   saltwater—
desire—
                   salt in the belly—

I check for the children this morning
        but remember they've been taken by Niccolò

to play at weighing rocks, to inspect facets slicing—

                (What is the price of one facet?—)

To study rocks the children will start
        ruby, opal, and sapphire adventures,

making ruby, opal, and sapphire luck—

                The price of one facet?—

What salt in the body— What gambles the earth—

On feast day at Piazza San Marco,

vendors cadge and cajole

and I buy spices, open my pouch

to let loose into the sun the mysterious thousand smiles

as if Buddha faces were ducats

making change.

Some day I'll turn with a smile as wind culls
                    the air to push sails across

the port with a thin whistle

and you'll know me better than a coin's spilling faces

simply to say something simple to each other

in the cloved breath that shapes a throat—

d. I am used to my desire

I could stand in an inland meadow and through my feet

feel the roots of grass knot

how early can the universe be?

I am used to my desire —

a napkin across my lap,

in the giant eye

I am not used to my desire.

the Blemmyae with faces

to meet the people who feed

We need desire to shape our death —

flower-patterned,

I mean the lover who takes you

and rosette underneath —

I wear wasps to barrette my hair —

I unfold it,

but too — it magnifies

of a grasshopper, but too —

Walk far to meet

stretched from their breasts,

only on the smell of apple —

I mean, a wisp of curtain,

thrown across the moon,

like the the roots of grass.

Across a finger's breadth of sheet between my knee and yours,

I am forever chasing you,

You're silent about the prison

but house arrest, shut

with Rustichello) but you've told

to Suzhou. Sitting in the parlor

and quills: the gryphon-bird

the Sciopod ran on its sole leg,

the country of only women —

who wanted these,

the fitful step

paper riffling, spices pestled —

between the roughest silences

you, gleaming,

direction a lie —

in Genoa (no iron bars

in a burnished parlor

much else, from here

with simple parchment

hoisted elephants in its talons,

the country of men with tails —

it was Rustichello

it was you who wanted

of cobblestones, sand, silk,

Direction is a slatch

as late at night in our bed,

hyphenate us —

I braid your hair

to shiver, brimming,

With a pestle and mortar,

Do I ever wish my choices

diminished, maybe?

less cross-hatched?—

of rose mary, for the tea

for the girl who would love

the boy to ride

toward unnumbered

in my hands

hear it growing.

one can let the light out of seeds.

more scrubbed—the glare more

Do we ever wish our hands

for the sheet, the cleansed fragrance

my fingers close around—

to twirl across calendars,

a dragon's neck

continents—seek

still warm from this cup.

The cant of your chin

is the trouble with desire,

feeding it *just*

first sip—I'll admit

of my own

off the bay

you can follow

the way

two parts curiosity—

the trouble is

enough—lips to rim,

I'm concubine to this,

minute, when a breeze

touches leaves into spangles—

yearning all

into me,

three parts wind—

Trees move houses past our windows on the way to Milan

Forest rain, a gauze   we could heal ourselves with,

asks no attention for itself,   stays patient.

The faces of saints rounded   as babies just before sleep,

not the same as the hushed   circle about the Khan

who allowed no shouting,   no talking, even,

from as far away   as the next town.

You're pleased our oldest girl   has drawn a map

complete with sea serpents   curled in two corners.

The mist turns my skin to dough,   giving me warm ideas:

if I were to look full at you   before the next town

attaches itself   to our window

I would not   know the way home —

e. By a dollop of moonlight become

The men huddle, velvet tunics, green feathers, maroon capes,

crowding the parlor in a semi-circle around Marco.

The mangonels catapult boulders. The drums—great naccaras

big as people—begin to beat, and viewing the battle from afar,

the Khan stands on a wooden platform shouldered

by four elephants, orders troops of 30,000 at a time.

As Marco speaks, the men in our parlor steam off their velvet shoulders.

The elephants barely shudder with each hit.

Sometimes I would like to feel singing dwindle to the tissue

of a single note, then not at all—What we say

is of the weightless part of us that we shed off our clothing.

Mangonels let loose their boulders—

the *whole heaven . . . canopied* with arrows—

A parrot on the Khan's wrist, green and turquoise and screaming.

The parlor reticulated with breaths.

When you talk I'm a song-tone in your sentence.

At the table I pour cream, study the minutes of your look

as you remember the Sa-Yan-Fu mangonels, the creases around

your mouth flaring with franchisement, still surprisingly young.

You helped the Mongols build them—European machines,

catapults, *capable of throwing stones of 300 pounds weight*

to attack any building made of alas, alas, one weed in the wall.

The city of Sa-Yan-Fu, receiving one missile,

immediately surrendered their gold-woven silks.

Polos and Mongols: did you stroke ink into a character

for Polos and Mongols against Chinese?

At night I am the clearest of your features, perhaps,

by a dollop of moonlight become Chinese—

City of 6,000 bridges, Suzhou doesn't need to haggle

for its sunbeams or its swaths of silk. In legends

the most beautiful girls—from Suzhou.

Our littlest daughter clutches at everything, lets drop even more,

owns the crown of your eyebrows. She assesses

her fisted noodles like you assess rubies.

At times I retell your expanding stories to myself—but I'm Chinese,

hidden among the wood pilings of Venice—

That's when you're gone.

When you return, gem-dazzle and smiles, I stop missing

my Suzhou sisters upon sisters, who I never thought to write—

The many hundred chimneys of Venice, goblet-shaped —

Sometimes I open, many-glassed and wide

as leaving parts of myself across a continent.

I would like to disguise myself as a continent.

Profiles of the family crumble to ovals, this evening the candle flame

grows orange petals. I'll sing lullabies to my Chinese daughters —

whom I remember, of course, are not Chinese,

though in the candlelight I'll sing them so, listen to the belly laugh you,

husband, throw over chimneys and balconies, your laugh pulsing

to the exact curve of each new daughter whom together we write.

The mangonel stories may be embellished.

Tiny grains of gravel funnel the pillow's ticking—

You sleep, and I see there's silver poured into your palm lines.

Departing geese—their flight might as well drain an ocean.

The mangonels catapult this story

while you sleep unaware of the crucible of your shoulders.

A camel hair needles the mattress.

For an hour tomorrow I'll be paralyzed remembering

what I will have tonight—

the dream in which I do not appear.

In China the Zardandan walk down pavement called *corn-ear cobbles*,

gather in mourning to burn fake money. We Venetians would never

burn money, even if it were made of paper, even if it were fake—

no matter how much we mourned.

European metal : Chinese paper

European dragon : Chinese dragon

Monsters at both ends of the Silk Road open their fanged maws—

One dragon blows fire, one dragon mouths the pearl of the world.

I mourn my past and future self who will never

know each other well enough—

dragon scales burn : empires burn empires :

we purchase a second—

f. After falling in the canal from reaching

I want to touch, in

paintings, the thick
platters of halos
worn by saints, so
this-rather-than-that
hatches.

This—safety:
that—out there.
Not at all like Mary's
cheekbones, mine are
sharp, needing.

You rest in their shadows,
while our middle daughter
nests in my lap
after falling in the canal
from reaching

between bridge spindles
for a duck's
rainbow feathers,
she wanted the glitters
in its wake—

her hair, drenched
then dried, embossed

an almost non-human
tangle. A moth gimbals
the lantern.

You touch her hair.

As women hang carpets on the balcony rails

my girl, inside,
hacks a briny
cough, I exist

to hear that cough,
her head across my knees.

She knows by heart
our houses' mossed,
mildewed ankles,

the waves dipping
cobalts, golds,
rusts, umbers

as rosetta beads

they bounce
the tides,
our roads.

Long sweep
along the jaw,

she focuses me.
I want to hold her

tighter than water—

Sewing will not thread

for me, the needle
itself wants to split

a thousand ways, I start

an embroidered lion,
thready mane,
no body.

In sleep now, my girl's
features pull
toward the center of her face.

I won't hang a carpet today,

we might drift away

everywhere
seas

suck at our walls—

The placed-here bed

and around it
we, its lashes,

because of the tonic,
because of the salve
and the other ways we pull

toward remembering. If
the world is shaken
then it's shaken,

sky under earth,
rain that falls up.

Sit with me a while,
would you?

I don't know if
facing south or east—

happenstance seats—
don't worry about that,

don't worry about faith,
about Milan,

or whatever that is in its place—

The Thousand Buddha Caves, westernmost

outpost of China, where
turquoise, after months
of eastward sliding
on Taklimakan sand,
almost took
your eyes out

with disbelief:
in hundreds of cave
paintings and statues,
the turquoise of an oasis

dreamed-and-found—
the Buddha face

not quite man or woman,

halos kinetic with
the movement of flying
beings, mermaid tails

of fastest silk
not ending
in aquamarine fins
but in an aquamarine
point

from which flight
emits.

Some heavens curl
with rewards,
some with ecstasies.

If Buddha had been
Christian, you say,
he'd have been a saint.
In the Thousand Buddha Caves

a mural of a crowd
shows one man,
a *round-eyes*,
painted in the middle:

a *round-eyes*, there
before you, Marco—

Our girl's aqua eyes
erase with sleep.

What you found finally to the east of the desert

in China: Suzhou, called
the *Venice of the East*,

our twin city, rounded
bridge to rounded
bridge, built of stone,

precious as silk and jade,
you came to love

but couldn't bring back.

We bridge over our plates,
neither of us can help
but skim a ledge or two,

and we wait
for the rest. Rest

a moment, breathe sky,
pilings steadying
themselves. No birds
trill, no ships slap by.

We have waited
for our girl's rippled
breath to even,
as still as the desire
to float

mirrors the arc
under rounded
bridges,

cinches

circle,
circle, circle,

and there are many—

The vendor near the campanile

sells glass figurines—
transparent trees, ships
spikey in the grasp.

I, Donata Badoer,
no curls glossed
as a blessed

madonna, no jade skin
as an Eastern empress,

sit to watch coins'
haloes and crosses
spark finger to finger,
give one to another's
rounding hands.

Carpets sail
on wrought balconies,
women look out
from behind them,
foreheads painted
by clouds. Days ago

my girl, canal-fevered
in her room, talked rapidly
of feathers' sparkly
turquoise and bright-black.
Today I left her

sleeping a nap smooth
and starred as Murano
glass. On a whim

I buy a glass ship rigged
with enameled bowsprit,
tiny, sharp gobbets for oars,

to skim
in the current of her palm.

g. The translation that loops

Venice's wine sea feeds wine fish

that wine gulls dive for,
regardless of us,

        you're restless
     as you leave me again today,
tacking in the direction of comfort,

toward Ponte delle Tette, Bridge of Open Blouses,

and I test repose in the hold of a wound

niched directly in blood waves pushing.

I need dressing for the promise-rips,
as when a girl I looked for Mary's nod
                to reassure —

as you look now for the nod, exotic, here in town

    that shows this street bending away, that one twisting,

this route carrying its far to farther —

When I try to translate

the water lappings in the canal, they turn
                              bland with shyness, turn

prow-first, the long massage, for the boats entering.

A vow: translation that loops, rips, laps,

                         where *could* lands a moment at the mount of a bridge?

A road commits at last to the dust around its prints.

Our pledge: untranslatable surf,

or the curling road a camel took to voices wisped in the Taklimakan,
the custom of the Taklimakan husband giving up his wife
                         for the night, to the traveler's caprice —

what caprice then might be wished
to blow our skin together,

the hours, Marco, when you're stranger and traveler to me —

We might choose a merriment:

wear a mask.
We could greet each other

      from behind bobbing feathers,
          so even the children wouldn't guess.

Yours, the usual costume of oarsman.

Mine, a change—I'll wear a *moretta* of black velvet
    sleeked with red plumes
        to hide in me all that loves blue.

Who knows but tonight the Pope himself
      might nod from behind a flamingo's swayings.

        Forgive the naughty.
I hold my face on by biting a button.

Inside the mask we'll smell paste and paper, and silence all night
        yet I'll take your hands with abandon.

What love we may pass in alleys, writhing in any shadow,
      what dealings—devil, medico—

may cross,
what demon may grip—

But in our new eyes we'll bring each other in.

Forgive my wanting your world touch.

We'll wear a mask, each,   of the other's face.

Thin veil of spit the cat applies to her body—

shapeless gestures our hands propose—

a gryphon stands on the street corner pedestal
       so that any ghost with death in its pocket
           will shrink back into pearl or eggshell,

some patch of white gleam on the sea swell—

the Ponte de le Somewhere trains the wet under it—
the Ponte de le Tell Me Something True doesn't—

as the cat jumps into its shadow, or the shadow into its cat—

perhaps form could make the wrong visit, after all,

perhaps edging closer—

You hold

       the brooch away from me—

I don't deserve it, you say—

       an emerald disc, your great aunt's, with sapphire leaves.

You're right, I don't want it—

          until now, and I seize—

      am I seizing?—

            Outside a broom switches the walk.

You don't move because you know: one hand is forward, one is back:

       our bodies square to each other:

my palm complicit with your cheek,
your arm under my breasts cinching me, I start
          to wrench toward you—

    we're in the middle of the room—

        my chest pinned—

I don't know how I came to this archway,

                rattling jewels—
      an echo works in a doorframe
           where I can hear myself
                  both leaving and returning.

You don't understand why women hold:

      a measure, a laugh, a lantern spilling flatness onto a deck
                with sharpening portent, or parting.

Stop talking to me in Rustichello's grammar.

I wonder why I try to speak above
        water stirring limbs and debris when water

can take us down to its town at the bottom—

A length of flexing bridges
          crawls with merchants walking over
        the tops of gondoliers' heads—

underneath, waves knead patiently.

h. The story's latitude

A lion lies down at the Khan's feet.

Remember when we used to think silk was combed
        from the leaves of trees?

             This morning the birds ride trees.

Especially fine is the silk from near the Yangtze, you said,
        enamored of its liquid mirrors.

The Khan's lion streaks *lengthways with white, black, and red stripes.*
Our lion holds his paw on an open book,

        looks over our city walls, which are water
           I melt to, I must remember at all times, walls of water—

           The cat watches at the speed of birds.

For silk, you must heat the cocoon till it gives its thread, finding

just the right heat— difficult—

        till it gives it easily.

The domed palace of the Khan

can be taken down like a tent. Pleasure of silk cords, cane rafters,

gold on the swaying walls. *The greatest palace that ever was*

is easy to move as whim. The dream in which I do not appear—

the dream you hold me tightest in—the desert all around—

the jade smooth as fingernails carving skin—

where I am. Where you hold me I end.

And the fabric thrown into

the fire to clean—does it smoke?

And the *stones that burn like logs*—how well can they warm arms

steaming in baths? In the desert you painted arrows on posts,

so when you woke in the morning you'd know which way to go.

Spirit voices ring in the spaces between bridge rails,

voices follow us today, like our cat stares centuries into the column

before she leaps to the window ledge.

How I'd love to think I anticipated you, Marco, but that thought

I may have to give up—To think that of the spirit voices,

it could have been my song, your ear—or that you knew futures

with my leaning in them, mixing lightest sand, or that I could stand

where the *spirit voices* that sewed bells around their lips came to—

You went, ruled

(or at least as one of the interlopers, you ruled—

as one of the *colored eyes*, foreigners),

charmed, thrived, returned—the story's line of latitude.

If one interlocutor were to ask my simple, spreading story—

but as soon as I think that, the story pulls to a thinness I can't see—

the reaching, rubbing feeling in my stomach—

I'm utterly nonnarrative, I'm where the baby pulls and in my core,

there's grip—

Slice the Tianjin pear,

find surprise at the white interior—and the Mongol court laughed

and you made a laugh—*white as dough inside*, fragrant as orchards.

I see one Tianjin pear—in the center of the Khan's mighty palace

sculpting shadows in every direction, shadows fluid on silk walls.

One Tianjin pear has not yet been cut—

i. Uncrumple more story

One can unscroll a map too far to retrace roads,

edges fray to purple ravens tumbling off thin ways,

fresh as spit and shiny,
Cathay, Colba, Guisay, Philistia.

Folds relax their creases,
breathe themselves to lake beds, river bottoms,

silt-softened, indecision-gentled.

Why would they care for east and southeast anymore?

Some days your hand on the cities loses its way, smoothes perspective

so that a town could wring an ocean, float a state.

Some days you hear desert voices *calling you by name,*
voices *the strains of many instruments*—

and I wonder, will you stay to watch the map's rivers branch to
grapevines that have their city in our campo,

where our little one wants to curl her hand around your finger?—

and will you bend,
to study the way of her face—

The goodness you don't need to prove

because goodness is not
        that different from curiosity for you—

You are curious where I feel random,
          the mending thread not yet put to service—

Year by year you uncrumple more story:

the emperor's brocaded sleeve gesturing to start the banquet,
the mare's milk turned to wine by the Khan's sorcerers,
tens of thousands of white horses never ridden,
falcons faster than sandstorms—

Out in our courtyard a petal catapults a bee from itself—

Our babies play tigers who hunch in chairs and cushions—

A cluster on the grapevine nods its chins at me—

      I can't tell you any of this—

Again you recount the events at Sa-Yan-Fu,

power slips on a blood floor,
visitors encourage with listening-grunts.

I dream: a veined light smearing a Venice dock.

You whisper that songs oar through desert sands, bracing and unbracing,
        the voices of companions
                who lure you from the oasis, out into the nothing

        where direction no longer wastes itself with apparatus.

I see three boats tied to a red Venice dock.

On your deathbed, asked to retract the fabrications in your book,

you'll say you had *not told even half* of what you'd seen.

I haven't told even half of that.

Out in the bay, boats

gather then fan—
canvas holds then slacks—

I brought pears from the market,

the girls sit on the bench and eat them,
                     the source of light leaking
               from every point I stop to consider.

Husband, match lips with mine—
pear, hum, the minute resting
                  in your wrist.
         This is the time

I might say your Mongol name
        and not notice how stringent it feels in my mouth,

my hand bunched as a country—
what day puts of the tree into our keeping—

Out in the bay waves parallel each other, perfumed hair.

Here, the pear is full of trees—

      The girls hold little moons so actual
              I feel the voids cut around them.

Poling past swans, the boatman pools

in white-ruffled reflections,
                I can't see his eyes.

Above him a wayfarer walks on cobbles, rolled bedding on his shoulder.

                I see his face, it says, *this way*—

perhaps the boat brings another visitor,
             come to ask Marco for advice about the road,

                face saying, *this way, and only this*—

The boatman disappears in white-pasted swan water.

Pretending they're winged horses, children by the fish market
                gallop and flap, their hair flashing blue.

Daytime moon, not quite full, sits in.

He was ready to come back—more than twenty years ready,
      the jewels in his hems heavy.

I was never ready but always wanting to start where water starts—

Notes

Almost no information exists about Donata Badoer, except that she married Marco Polo after he returned to Venice and they had three daughters: Fantina, Bellela, and Moreta.

Information about Polo was taken from many different sources, especially the following:

Travels of Marco Polo, Ernest Rhys, Editor, J. M. Dent and Sons, 1918. Italicized phrases are taken from this source.

Marco Polo: The Description of the World, Sharon Kinoshita, Hackett Publishing, 2016.

Marco Polo and the Discovery of the World, John Larner, Yale University Press, 1999.

"Marco Polo in China," Mike Edwards, *National Geographic*, 6 June, 2001.

The Mysteries of the Marco Polo Maps, Benjamin B. Olshin, The University of Chicago Press, 2014.

Etruscan Press Is Proud of Support Received From

Wilkes University

Youngstown State University

The Raymond John Wean Foundation

The Ohio Arts Council

The Stephen & Jeryl Oristaglio Foundation

The Nathalie & James Andrews Foundation

The National Endowment for the Arts

The Ruth H. Beecher Foundation

The Bates-Manzano Fund

The New Mexico Community Foundation

Founded in 2001 with a generous grant from the Oristaglio Foundation, Etruscan Press is a nonprofit cooperative of poets and writers working to produce and promote books that nurture the dialogue among genres, achieve a distinctive voice, and reshape the literary and cultural histories of which we are a part.

Books from Etruscan Press

etruscan press

www.etruscanpress.org

Etruscan Press books may be ordered from

Consortium Book Sales and Distribution

800.283.3572

www.cbsd.com

Etruscan Press is a 501(c)(3) nonprofit organization.
Contributions to Etruscan Press are tax deductible
as allowed under applicable law.
For more information, a prospectus,
or to order one of our titles,
contact us at books@etruscanpress.org.